# MY LUCKY DOG

## Mellon Tytell

*wm*

WILLIAM MORROW
*An Imprint of* HarperCollins*Publishers*

HarperCollins books may be purchased for educational, business, or sales promotional use. For information please write: Special Markets Department, HarperCollins Publishers, 10 East 53rd Street, New York, NY 10022.

FIRST EDITION

Designed by Mellon Tytell

Library of Congress Cataloging-in-Publication Data is available upon request.

ISBN 978-0-06-147307-4

08  09  10  11  12   ID/TOPPAN   10  9  8  7  6  5  4  3  2  1

3 2530 60617 7796

*For John Tytell, my love at first sight*

There is no love. There are only acts of love.

—Denis Diderot

It was the best time of my life.

A young boy put a picture of Hunter in
the window of a pet store in Vermont.
His dog was up for adoption.
I was the only one who called.

We brought him back to our
house on Colvin Hill Road in Danby.
In the thirteen years we had him we
never had to say B-A-D D-O-G.

He had been kept in a kennel for six weeks.
The minute he arrived home, he curled up in
his crate and heaved a giant sigh of relief.

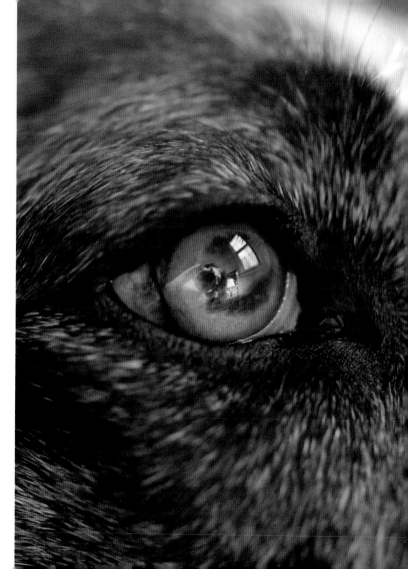

"Your dog is a little wild," said a neighbor to my husband, John.

But he didn't have a mean bone in his body.

He liked to sleep late.

People always tried to guess Hunter's breed.
Some said he ran like a greyhound.
"A hundred miles an hour," said a kid.

Hunter was in love with Byron. It was mutual.

Hunter's other home was in Greenwich Village. But when he was eleven years old, he became unable to walk up the two flights of stairs to our apartment.

We moved to Vermont.

Fortunately, I found Dr. Linda Squires, who came over every week to treat him with acupuncture. Soon Hunter was able to trot to the crest of the hill, a good half a mile away.

I think Hunter missed the City too.

He enjoyed exploring the urban landscape, especially the art scene in Chelsea.

Some friends and family called me naïve and silly for giving up my husband, career, and social life to take care of a dog. After all, I had a show and a book published that year.

But when the planes were striking the Twin Towers,
John, Hunter, and I were in the pumpkin patch on our neighbor's farm
down the road. John had decided to take a sabbatical to be with us.

Every day we would take long hikes.
Hunter barked at the cows,
but they couldn't care less.

Time passed.

Hunter became a grand old man.

Though the hardships of growing old were now reflected in his eyes.

He could no longer sit. His spinal cord wasn't sending messages to his paws.

Before, he would run up the road to visit Byron. All I needed to do was turn on the old Honda and he came flying home.

Dressing up was something he adored.

I knew that Hunter would leave me for any man who walked into the room.

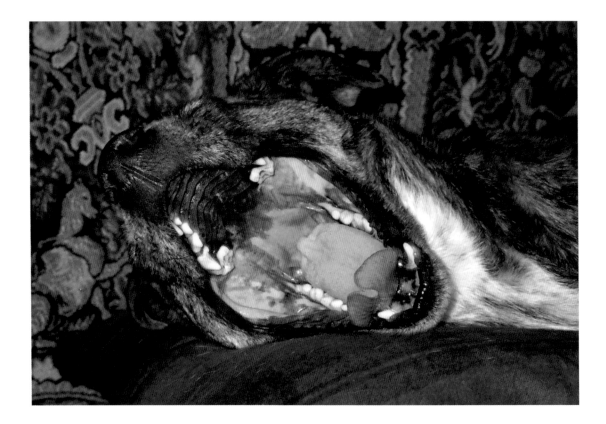

But I was madly in love with him.

To me, Hunter was more fascinating than a Pollock or Picasso.

He was a good sport, always tolerating
my obsession with taking pictures of him.

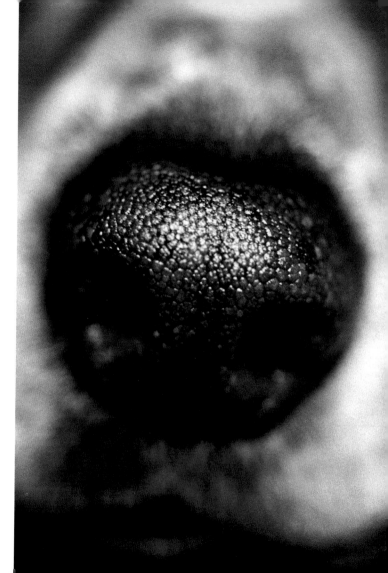

His fur smelled of pine trees and wild roses.

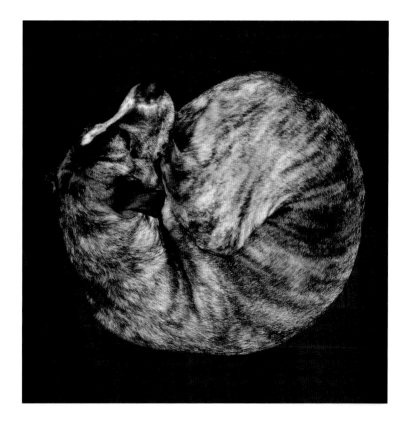

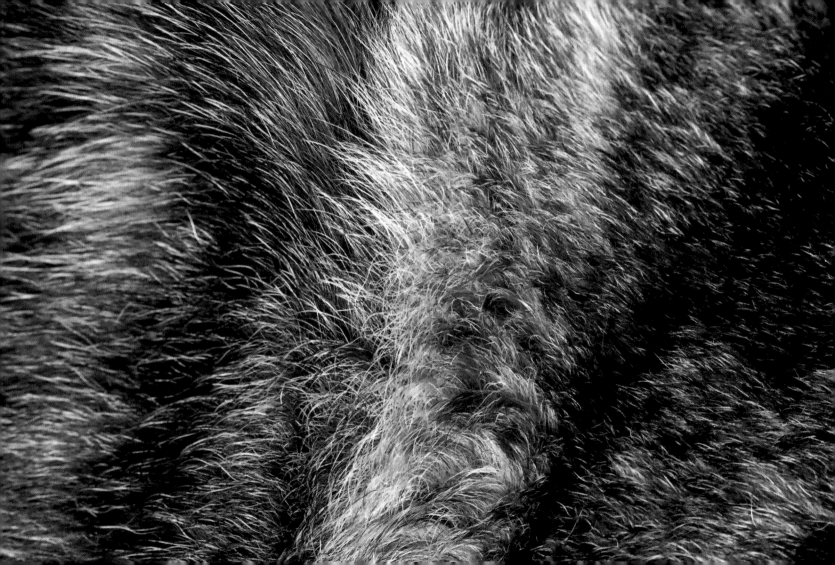

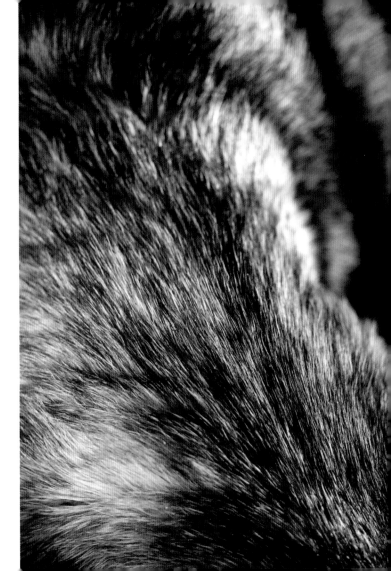

His final winter was one of the coldest and snowiest on record.

We walked around the house and invented new games.

He never complained.

He waited until springtime to leave me.

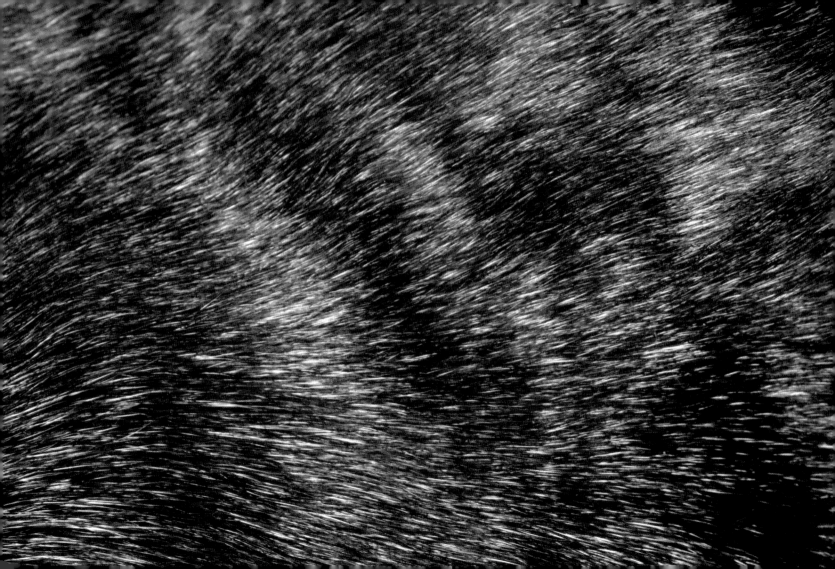

Hunter's last supper was grilled chicken, basmati rice, broccoli, fruit cocktail, and a raspberry ice pop.
He left me for good a few hours later.

I remember Hunter every May before the dandelion down is scattered by the wind.

The day after Hunter died a yellow warbler
appeared outside my window and sang for days.

# ACKNOWLEDGMENTS

*So I said I love you and I love what you do*
*Come on do your thing*
    —Mike Heron, The Incredible String Band

*My Lucky Dog* was blessed by the loving commitment of many people. I am deeply grateful to everyone who contributed to making this book a reality.

Tom Ridinger's curatorial eye helped me whittle down hundreds of images, and his design expertise was crucial to the project. I couldn't wish for a more dedicated friend. I owe a particular debt to friend Joyce Johnson, whose clarity of mind and literary skills enabled me to put words to paper. Mike Perkins provided invaluable assistance with technical skill, enthusiasm, and patience. Always lovingly generous, my soul brother Alan Maltz has been a constant source of visionary insights, unwavering support, and humor. Besides allowing me unlimited access to his darkroom, Terry Niefield has for decades shared his deep well of photographic knowledge. My most enduring source of devotion has been my husband, John Tytell.

I am profoundly thankful to gifted coeditor, publicist, and friend Dee Dee DeBartlo; she believed in

*My Lucky Dog* from the beginning. Dee Dee's keen sensibility and spontaneous decisions are amazing. It's a great honor to have Laurie Chittenden as editor; so intelligent and thoughtful, she knows what to add, remove, and move, truly enhancing the work. Additional and invaluable assistance was provided to me by the great team at William Morrow: Will Hinton, helpful and calm; Michael Conroy, for his precise instructions about the process of publishing; James Houston, Ervin Serrano, and Emily Fink, available, cheerful, and kind. Appreciation goes to Steve Schaub of Indian Hill Gallery for his excellent scans and untiring dedication to finishing the job in a timely manner.

I am deeply thankful to Robert Frank and June Leaf, master mentors, for their encouragement, wisdom, and friendship on the road. With extreme kindness, Peter MacGill assisted at every opportunity.

A heartfelt thanks to Elly Davis, the definition of a true friend, who gave me unwavering encouragement and was always there for me. To Dr. Linda Squires, veterinarian with a giant heart; I will treasure the memory of you coming to my house in blizzards and ice storms to treat Hunter, as well as becoming a forever friend. Gratitude and thanks to my neighbors and friends, salt of the earth, Barbara and Tommy Shimaitis, Kay and Chip Wright, Jay Venable and Annette Smith, who looked after me when I was alone on the mountain. Heartfelt thanks to the caring family of Irma and Ron Nagle, for giving me the opportunity to adopt Hunter; Quincy Shaw, veterinarian, who did emergency surgery on Hunter in my living room; Dr. Jay Kuhlman, who took wonderful care of Hunter in the city, and never failed to return my calls. Loyal friends Bob Charde, Holly George-Warren, Deb and Ken Stuart, and Tamara Weiss always embraced my ideas with positivity. Many thanks to attorneys extraordinaire, Michael Miller, Lucas Ferraro, and Raymond Dowd; I value their kindness and generosity.

I owe a lot to the people who gave me a lucky opportunity in life. To Tosh Matsumoto, where I had my first taste of a photography studio; to Jay Maisel, first teacher, whose staff members, Josh and Peter, continue to offer their help; Ralph Lauren, whose risk in hiring a beginner launched my career; Claire Devener for sending me on location to the Amazon and enlarging my scope. I will always be grateful to Marge Neikrug, who first exhibited my photography and urged me on energetically. Appreciation goes to Klaus Moser, master printer; Rochelle Ratner for teaching me about the computer over the phone; to Jack Barlev at Spectra, John Conte of Advanced Imaging, and Terrence Thomas of Century Copy.

Finally, *My Lucky Dog* is a tribute to the beloved departed in my life, those souls who left an indelible imprint, and who will always have a treasured place in my heart: for my known father, the artist Leon Gregori, who helped develop my "eye" and exposed me to the magic of art; for my unknown father, Maurice Quint, who had an osmotic influence on my being; for Lazar Kirshner, my beloved grandfather, who took me blueberry picking and taught me to love nature; my long departed friend, Dennis Lublin, who first introduced me to photography; Josef Breitenbach, Weegee, Ernst Haas, each in their way affecting my vision; for the rare compassion of Richard Hire; for the magical friendship of Kazuko; to Richard Palmer, my dearest high school friend, whose precocious vision taught me to live a life of truth and passion; and, last, for my cherished Hunter, my muse and teacher, tenderly cheering me on along the way.